B•Y•G•O•N•E

Arthur's Hill & Westgate

by

A.D. Walton

Published by

Newcastle Libraries
& Information Service

Acknowledgments:

The author would like to thank several people for information: Noel Hanson and Barry Redfern, and in particular Alec Campbell author of *High Elswick a Hundred Years Ago* (written to celebrate the centenary of St Philip's Parish Church consecrated in 1873).

Photographic acknowledgments:

All photographs are copyright of West Newcastle Local Studies except for the following:
9: copyright of Norman McCord;
2, 14, 21: copyright of Newcastle Libraries & Information Service.

ISBN: 1 85795 084 4

City of Newcastle upon Tyne,
Education & Libraries Directorate,
Newcastle Libraries & Information Service,
1998

Front cover:

The original buildings of Newcastle Union Workhouse, built from 1840 on Westgate Road, are in the right background and are now part of Newcastle General Hospital. The Workhouse three-storey lodge, left, was built in 1882 and partly demolished in 1939 as a wartime precaution. Horse trams ran before 1901 when electric trams were introduced and the route here would be down Westgate Road and then on to Grey's Monument. The horse and cart, right, are on the corner of Brighton Grove.

For your information …

Copies of photographs which are copyright of Newcastle Libraries & Information Service may be ordered and purchased from the Local Studies Section, Newcastle City Library.

Contact West Newcastle Local Studies at Benwell Library, Atkinson Road, Newcastle upon Tyne NE4 8XS.

Also by A.D. Walton:
Bygone Westgate Road, £1.50

City Tours visit the City and suburbs during the Summer months. A free brochure is available from the City and Tourist Information Service, Newcastle City Library.

A free brochure detailing other local history publications is also available from Newcastle City Library.

For information on any of the above contact

Publications
City Library
Princess Square
Newcastle upon Tyne
NE99 1DX

or telephone 0191 261 0691 ext. 232.

I first became interested in local history as a schoolboy, living at 73 Brighton Grove. There were many reminders of the recent past there, such as the old-fashioned bellpulls in the house, and I knew that it had once stood in a field instead of surrounded by terraces as it was then, in the 1930s.

A walk along Fenham Road and Philip Street took me via Monday Street and Seaham Street to my school in Bath Lane – Rutherford College Boys' School. We later moved to 4 Brighton Grove where my mother opened a ladies' outfitters (now a launderette). Opposite were the east walls of Newcastle Union Workhouse, then the Wingrove Hospital, which in 1900 had been the west boundary to the built-up area north of Westgate Road.

In the 1930s our lives were usually circumscribed by the situation of our home, school, church, work and the local picture house. My world was Arthur's Hill and Westgate, from the hospital to Bath Lane and between Barrack Road and Westgate Road.

At this time we sometimes called our part of Westgate Road the Turnpike, even though it had been built in 1741 and was only listed as such on maps until the mid-19th century. North of the turnpike was known as North Elswick, and the area nearer the town as Westgate, until the 1820s. When Westgate and Elswick townships became part of Newcastle in 1835 there were buildings on either side of Westgate Hill, joined on the west by the 1826 estate of Isaac Cookson opposite the nonconformist Westgate Cemetery. Cookson named the estate after his son Arthur and the first streets were named after his other sons: John, Edward and William. Further up the turnpike road the O.S. map for 1859 shows only John Dobson's Prospect House and Gloucester House before the Union Workhouse is reached. North to Barrack Road was mainly agricultural land.

The progress of the Industrial Revolution brought, in the mid-19th century, an urgent need for homes for the urban working class beyond the town boundaries. How the problem was solved in this densely crowded area can be seen in aerial photograph no. 9. Houses were cheaply erected at maximum speed on a geometrical pattern. The two-storey Tyneside flats lacked baths and inside toilets and the front doors opened straight onto the public street. The roads were cobbled and even after World War II lighting was still by gas. However, there was a strong community spirit, and as the late, well-loved, author and entertainer Joe Ging stated: 'If the area hadn't had discipline it would have sunk without trace.'

Present residents of the area might like to know the derivation of some of the street names. Near the Westgate Road high-rise flats, built on the site of Cookson's Estate, there are still Cookson Street and Place as well as Edward Place. Todd's Nook (the school was demolished in 1998) took its name from an early farm on Barrack Road situated near the bottom of the present Stanhope Street. There is still a Spring Garden Lane near the site of the farm, recalling the Spring Gardens of the 18th century where weekly concerts were held. At New Mills there was once a corn mill.

Much of the land between New Mills and Westgate Road was inherited by Rev. W.N. Darnell in the early 19th century. He was made Rector of Stanhope by Bishop Barrington. Though the Darnell pub was demolished in 1997 there remains Darnell Place, Stanhope Way and Street as well as Barrington Place. A few houses of the original Philip Street still exist, named after Darnell's nephew, Philip, and there is now a Philip Place. When St Philip's Church was built in memory of Archbishop Longley it stood in Longley Street, part of which still exists. The listed building now stands among new houses in St Philip's Close.

1. The centre building at 103 Westgate Rd stood between Pink Lane off left and Thornton St, right, with part of the Tyne Theatre (then Stoll Cinema) showing. It was a police and fire station between 1885 and 1933 and the scaffolding in front in 1936 indicates that it is about to be demolished so that the Essoldo Cinema can be built (1936-1986), succeeded by the Cannon until 1989. After demolition of the latter archaeologists were able to investigate a site where the Town Wall crossed the Roman Wall. In 1998 the future use of the site is uncertain.

2. The Stoll Picture Theatre address was 111 Westgate Rd and the date here is 1928. Originally the Tyne Theatre between 1867 and 1919, it then became the first cinema in Newcastle to show talking pictures. From 1974 the original name was revived. On its right can be seen part of the Pavilion Cinema (1917-1975) which was demolished in 1992 to be replaced by a building for elderly Chinese. The Waterloo Hotel on the right was the site of the new Tyneside Foyer, built by the Salvation Army as a centre for 16-25 year olds.

3. This building lay behind the Pavilion Theatre, mentioned in the previous view, in Temple St which runs from Blenheim St to Peel Lane. Here, in 1908, it was known as Temple St Methodist Mission. The building was erected as a synagogue and the plaque at the top reads 'Jews Synagogue: erected Sept XIX : VD XC VIII' ie AD 1838. The building was demolished in the 1920s and the plaque was then given to the local Jewish community. Within recent years it was removed from a Jewish cemetery and placed in front of Gosforth Synagogue.

4. The Bath Lane Congregational Church on the corner of Corporation St and Bath Lane was opened in 1860 for the preacher, doctor and educationalist John Hunter Rutherford. By the time of this 1982 photograph it had stood empty since 1939 when it was replaced by the opening of the West End Congregational Church, Two Ball Lonnen. The building behind was Rutherford College Boys' School between 1894 and 1957 before its transfer to the West Road. Before demolition in 1987 it had at one time been occupied by the College of Arts and Technology.

5. This photograph from c.1950 shows the North Elswick or Gallowgate pit belonging to the Elswick Coal Co. Ltd as seen from Diana St. The road ahead was Colliery Lane and was part of the route I took to Rutherford Boys' School in the 1930s via Seaham St to Bath Lane. The pit was worked from 1881 by the coal company and Colliery Lane led to the Low Elswick or Beaumont Pit near Scotswood Rd. The latter was closed during World War II and the Gallowgate Pit worked intermittently until the 1970s, with the site being cleared c.1980. Perhaps the date here can be reckoned by the Morris Eight car. The view from Diana St today shows the boundary wall of land owned by Newcastle Breweries.

6. This c.1906 meeting of the Spring Blossom Juvenile Temple of the Independent Order of Good Templars is being held in Derby St Methodist Church. Derby St ran between Diana St and Barrack Rd. The building ended its days in the 1960s as a Jewish Reform Synagogue. Thomas ('Daddy') King was the main temperance advocate of the area and he sits behind the pulpit rail at right. This is probably a prelude to a lecture on the evils of strong drink with the aid of the nearby blackboard on which is listed the constituents of a pint of beer.

7. The main buildings in this 1897 view have now been replaced by the Sutton Estate (once Sutton Dwellings) on the corner of Barrack Road and New Mills. Ahead on the right is Newcastle (later known as Fenham) Barracks with part of Temple Leazes lower right. The large building was occupied by Robert Jefferson, builder of nearby Jefferson St, with the address listed as Todd's Nook. It is probable that it was previously occupied by the agent for a group of houses to the rear called Barrack Square which were built to house soldiers' families and retired soldiers from the Barracks on the opposite side of Barrack Rd. By the time they were demolished these houses were in a poor condition.

8. The south-west corner of Fenham Barracks is on the left and to the right is Brighton Grove and then Nuns Moor Park. The date is 1906 as the tram service started in 1907 and no lines are discernible. Tram no. 12 is standing at the Hunters Rd terminus of a route which will take it through Spital Tongues to the Central Station. Driver Harding of 196 Stanhope St smiles at the small boy in his pedal car. Today we would see BBC Radio Newcastle on the left.

9. Looking east c.1950. From left to right in the foreground are the terraces of Arthur's Hill still standing, parts of Tamworth Road, Stanton St and Beaconsfield St. The grid pattern of terraces with Todd's Nook School on the left were built, starting in 1865, to the design of the basic Tyneside flat. Street names included Philip, Monday, Jefferson, Hamilton, Stanhope, Darnell, Avison, Moor and Hindhaugh. During the 1970s these streets were demolished and replaced by modern estates with garden-like surroundings.

10. A view from the Douglas Terrace side of Snow St School in 1978. It was one of the first three permanent schools set up by Newcastle School Board after the 1870 Education Act and was opened in 1875 to accommodate 1000. At one period it was called Arthur's Hill Board School, with baths and wash-house adjoining. I was taught swimming here when we came as a class from Rutherford School, and I often called in afterwards at a corner shop for a packet of broken biscuits. Pupils were transferred to Moorside Community School in 1981, the building demolished and the site grassed over. Cookson Close and Edward Place, off right, give reminders of the original Arthur's Hill estate names.

11. St Philip's Church was built in memory of Archbishop Longley, founder of the Lambeth Conference and was consecrated in 1873. William Edward Moll, shown here, was the third vicar (1893-1925) and among his many contributions to people in the parish was the turning of the parish hall into a cinema popularly known as the 'Cosy', after 1908. The church building is now occupied by a religious organisation.

12. These are some of the original houses of the Arthur's Hill estate built by Isaac Cookson from 1826 and named after his son Arthur. The streets were named after his other sons John, Edward and William and this view shows a back lane with 3 Back Edward Street on the left and the rear of William Street on the right. The arch for horse traffic opens under no. 330 Westgate Road with the wall of the 1829 Westgate Cemetery clearly visible on the opposite side of the main thoroughfare. After this photograph was taken in 1937 for compulsory purchase purposes, the houses were demolished and prefabricated dwellings built on the site followed by blocks of flats.

13. A view of Beaconsfield St from Westgate Rd c.1910. The houses were built about 1880 when they ended at Longley St. Those on the left were demolished in 1980 to form the boundary of a grassed over area adjacent to Westgate Hill School. In this photograph it would appear that the children had been carefully posed to straddle the road before the slow approach of the horse.

14. The tram on Westgate Rd in 1910 is opposite the top of Stanton St on the right. The front of Westgate Hill School caretaker's house and playground is a little further ahead up the road. In April 1980 I visited Jobling and Ellen Brown in their grocer's shop on the corner of Stanton St at 392 Westgate Rd. The business was called Grout and Brown and I watched it being emptied before demolition and clearance for Westgate Hill School recreation area extension. The school celebrated its centenary in 1998 to coincide with the date in the brickwork.

15. This street party for VE day 1945 was held in Tamworth Rd just behind Westgate Hill School. At the end of the table beyond the girl in the white hat is a wartime air raid shelter and further ahead is the main thoroughfare of Stanhope St. The Tamworth Road houses on the right corner were demolished about 1980 and the adjacent area grassed over.

16. James Smith stands in front of his wireless and bicycle shop at 263a Stanhope St in the 1930s. The shop was later extended to take over the whole corner with Stanton St. Note the posters below the window reading 'Accumulators charged here'. In 1998 no. 263 is owned by Milligans the bakers but for a very long time a large poster above the shop still advertised Smith's Bicycles.

17. The length of the women's skirts helps to date this scene to just before the First World War and the tram fittings confirm this. Crossley Terrace is in the foreground with Stanhope Street beyond, in the middle of a heavily populated area. According to Reid's map of 1885 the buildings off left on the corner of Brighton Grove are some of the first to be built in that street. Before the end of the 19th century every street, including Sidney Grove and Gainsbro' Grove further to the west, had been built up.

18. George Duncan owned a number of shops in Elswick, Benwell and Arthur's Hill in the 1920s and this view dates from around 1920. Delivery boys would carry baskets or push the large-wheeled barrow taking goods to the surrounding dwellings, some flats and some two-storey houses. This shop was at 16 Fenham Rd, on the corner of Dilston Rd left, and is now a post office.

19. Nuns Moor Park was formed from part of the Nuns Moor in 1887. This photograph shows the Brighton Grove entrance to the park during the 1920s with the park keeper's house. The gas lamp on the arch marks the entrance to Bird Cage Walk, leading on to a path between moor and allotments which met at Fenham Hall Drive. In the early part of the century many took this route from their crowded terraces to the fields of Fenham and then past Fenham Hall to the countryside beyond.

20. In 1839 the Newcastle Board of Guardians commenced to buy land on Westgate Rd in order to build a Union Workhouse to accommodate the residents of the four Poor Law Houses in Newcastle parishes. Buildings were erected by 1861 and this is the east wall on Brighton Grove, at one time the view from my bedroom window. Cycling clubs were very popular before the First World War and the nearby Dilston Road church had many activities for its young people. Here the church cycling club prepares for a ride into the country hoping the roads would be better for riding on than the cobbles and the tramlines near the tram terminus.

21. This small building used to jut out into Westgate Rd opposite the Wingrove, now General, Hospital and between the top of Bentinck Rd and Dunholme Rd. I remember it in the 1930s when it was a joiner's workshop. Thomas Oliver's map of 1844 names the road Turnpike Road and the building as the Toll House. An 1861 map gives it the name North Elswick Cottage. It was demolished around 1939. Beyond it can be seen the combined police and fire station named Arthur's Hill Station when opened in 1891 for the Westgate Division of the Newcastle Borough Police, with accommodation for six married men and a fireman on the premises. It was closed in 1965 and replaced with a new police station on the same site. This photograph was taken in 1907.